EVERYDAY HEROES
Overcome Challenges

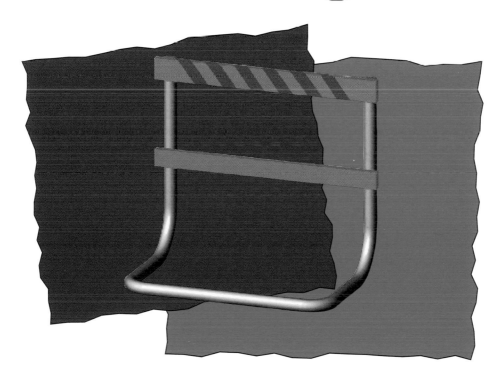

By Jill C. Wheeler

Published by Abdo & Daughters, 4940 Viking Drive, Suite 622, Edina, Minnesota 55435.

Copyright © 1996 by Abdo Consulting Group, Inc., Pentagon Tower, P.O. Box 36036, Minneapolis, Minnesota 55435 USA. International copyrights reserved in all countries. No part of this book may be reproduced in any form without written permission from the publisher.

Printed in the United States.

Edited By Julie Berg

Library of Congress Cataloging-in-Publication Data

Wheeler, Jill C., 1964-
      Everyday Heroes Overcome Challenges / Jill C. Wheeler
        p. cm. -- (Everyday Heroes)
      Includes index.
      Summary: Describes the active lives of a blind girl, boy with cerebral palsy, and three other disabled young people.
       ISBN 1-56239-700-1
      1. Handicapped youth--United States--Case studies--Juvenile literature. 2. Handicapped teenagers--United States--Case studies--Juvenile literature. [1. Physically handicapped.]
      I. Title
      HV1569. 3. Y68W54 1996
      362.4' 092'273--dc20
      [B]

96-7355
                                         CIP
                                         AC

Contents

It's What You Can Do, Not What You Can't

In summer 1995, 14-year-old Lisamaria Martinez applied for a summer job. She went through a special program that helps young people get jobs.

Lisamaria waited and waited for her job. Finally, the people at the program called Lisamaria's mother. They asked her what work Lisamaria could do. Her mother was quick to answer. "She can do everything she wants to do. Except read print."

Lisamaria is blind. She lost her sight when she was just five years old. Eventually, she convinced the people at the jobs program that she could work. They gave her a job helping children. The children loved Lisamaria. She did her job perfectly.

For Lisamaria, it was just one more success in a life filled with accomplishments. For the people at the jobs program, it was an education. They learned that people with a disability can be as active and involved as anyone else.

You may have kids with disabilities in your own class. It's important to remember that even though they're different from you, they're also a lot like you. They have many of the same interests. They have many of the same questions. They may not do some things as well as you do. They may do some things better than you.

Just as everyone is different, everyone has different levels of ability. What's important is to use whatever abilities you have to the fullest. This book looks at five young people who are doing just that. They have not let disabilities set them back. They are heroes that have overcome challenges themselves to help others.

In the last chapter of this book, you'll learn more about what it's like to have a disability. You'll also learn a new way of looking at people who have disabilities. Sometimes a little understanding is all it takes to be a hero yourself.

Lisamaria Martinez

Lisamaria Martinez's schedule would wear anyone out. The Oceanside, California, high school freshman is a blue belt in judo. She plays the violin and as an 8th grader, ran on the school track team. She writes poetry and short stories and reads many, many books. She received her school's Orchestra Award and All-Around Girl Award.

She did all of this and more without seeing a thing.

Lisamaria was only five years old when a rare syndrome robbed her of her sight. At first, she had to wear special goggles since her eyes could not make tears. The other children at her school laughed at her funny-looking goggles. Sometimes they played tricks on her.

Lisamaria found plenty of support from her family. They encouraged her to keep doing whatever she wanted. That's just what she did.

In second grade, Lisamaria entered a special contest for people who read braille. Braille is a method of reading for people who have problems seeing. The method uses bumps for letters instead of print. That way people can read with their fingers. The contest challenged readers to read as many braille pages as they could. Lisamaria won the contest for her age group. She read 2,081 pages in just three months!

Lisamaria also was active in her local Brownies troop. It gave her a chance to help others. She volunteered to collect canned goods for a local homeless shelter. She also

Lisamaria (right) took third place in the Judo National Competition.

visited elderly people in the hospital. Those actions earned her several awards. The Kiwanis organization gave her their Hope of America Award. The state of California also gave her the Jefferson Awards for Students for her work helping others. She and her mother flew to Washington, D.C., to receive the award from Barbara Bush.

In summer 1995, Lisamaria took on a new challenge. She entered the judo nationals competition and took third place. She also continues to compete in the Special Blind Olympics. There, she runs in the 50-, 100-, 200-, and 220-yard dashes. She also throws the shot put, runs the obstacle course and does both the high and long jumps.

Lisamaria often surprises people with what she can do without her sight. "I tell people there's nothing that stops me from doing anything," she says. "Just because I can't see doesn't mean I can't do anything. I do anything I want to. If I can't, I find a way."

Lisamaria plans to go to college and become a writer. She also loves to sing and would enjoy becoming a professional violinist. She's even taken special courses to learn how to live and travel independently.

One thing is for sure. Whatever she decides to do, she will.

"I do anything ...... I want to. ...... If I can't, I find a way."

Robert Keck

Robert Keck likes to ski, ride horses, and play soccer. Those aren't unusual interests for a 15-year-old. What is unusual is that Robert has cerebral palsy. A doctor told Robert's mother that Robert would never walk. Robert also has a learning disability. The disability occurred because Robert received too little oxygen before he was born.

Robert hasn't let any of those things stop him from doing what he wants. Today, he does walk using special canes. He also enjoys collecting sports cards. He plays video games and listens to music.

He is very active in sports, too. He plays on an adapted sports team in his

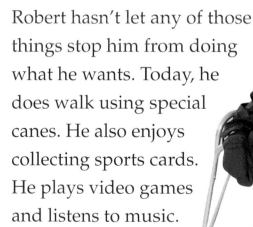

hometown of Hopkins, Minnesota. The team plays soccer, baseball, and hockey. In 1994, the team won the state title in hockey and baseball. In 1995, they won the state title in soccer. The players use wheelchairs and slightly different rules to play the game. They compete against other adapted teams.

Robert also enjoys downhill skiing. He uses special skis that work with a walker. "Each year I had to go and get pledges for a fund-raiser," he recalls. "One year I had to ski down the hill 10 times. My goal was to do 20. It was really cold. Most people had already gone inside. But my friends and family had pledged me. I kept going until I met my goal." Robert's work that day earned him Skier of

Opposite page: Robert with a Courage Center volunteer.

Robert enjoys horseback riding.

the Year honors for 1990. The award was given through Courage Center, a local organization that helps people with disabilities. Robert received special therapy from Courage Center. The therapy helped him learn to walk with crutches. He's lead a fuller life thanks to that.

"When I was a baby I was very weak," he says. "I had to have therapists help me learn to do even simple things. Like picking up a ball or moving my hands and arms. I took my first steps when I was six. That was using a walker. When I was 11, I learned to walk with crutches."

Robert's mother says these challenges have made him very understanding. "Robert knows what it's like to be left out," she says. "Kids would play with his toys. But they wouldn't let him play. He can really tell how other people are feeling."

Robert plans to go to college. Someday he hopes to open his own sports card shop. He encourages all young people to follow their dreams.

"Never give up," he says. "If you give up, you'll regret it later in life. Never say I can't, either. Keep trying. And don't let people tell you that you can't do something just because you have a disability. Tell yourself that you can do it if you want."

"If you give up, you'll regret it later in life."

Caya Consunji

Carmen "Caya" Consunji was five years old before she heard her name. She was seven before she could say it correctly. Today, the high school senior prefers to go by Caya. In Filipino, Caya means "You can do it." That's exactly the attitude Caya has taken.

Caya was born with a severe to profound hearing loss in both ears. Her family moved to the United States from their native Philippines when Caya was just four years old. Suddenly, Caya had to adjust to a new culture. She also began years of speech therapy to make herself understood by the rest of the world.

"Surviving every day in the hearing world is my greatest accomplishment," Caya says. "I had a difficult time in high school because they don't have any deaf support. Also, I am the first girl to attend my school. The students and teachers didn't know how to deal with deaf people, either. I had to work very hard in the classes and on the basketball court. I had to be very patient and to forgive the ignorant people who were scared of me because I was deaf."

Despite those challenges, Caya has excelled. She is on academic scholarship and the honor roll at her school. She won a silver medal in a national Latin exam. She received a President Bush Academic Excellence Award. Sports Illustrated featured her as a Junior Golf Scholarship awardee for the Chrysler Junior Golf Scholarship Program. She has played varsity basketball and softball in her hometown of Redwood City, California.

Additionally, she is a volunteer for the peer leadership program at her high school. She also has volunteered for the United Nations and a local daycare center. In 1995, Miss America, Heather Whitestone, chose Caya as one of 75 outstanding hearing-impaired students to receive Whitestone's Star Award. Whitestone also is hearing impaired.

Caya's favorite community service is helping the deaf. Now she is working with the Alexander Graham Bell

Association (AGBA) to start an affiliate in the Philippines. The AGBA helps people with hearing impairments. Caya has traveled to the Philippines as an AGBA ambassador and has helped with the AGBA scholarship program. She's also spoken at schools for the deaf and at events to raise money to help deaf people. In 1994, Caya was a guest speaker at the Fourth Asian-Pacific Congress on Deafness in Manila, the Philippines.

Caya's work earned her the Ninoy Aquino Memorial Award for Youth Achievement. It is the highest honor a Filipino-American can receive for community service. The award was named after slain Philippine Senator, Ninoy Aquino. Ninoy's wife, Corazon Aquino, became the first woman president of the Philippines.

Caya plans to attend college after she graduates from high school. She encourages all young people to continue learning. "It's never too late to learn something new," she says. "It's all right to ask for help when you need it. Don't get embarrassed to let people know how they can help you. Remember, if you don't ask for help, then you won't get it. If you have a goal or a dream, work hard for it and be patient. Don't give up trying."

"It is very difficult to overcome any disability," Caya says. "But believe me, you can do it." She adds, "Love, laws and technology empower the disabled."

For young people who can hear, Caya asks that they be patient and understanding when meeting a hearing-impaired person. "Being deaf is very hard," she says. "You may feel you're having a hard time communicating with the deaf. However, a deaf person has to work twice as hard to listen to you. Communication works when both people listen."

"You can do it."

Gina Jalbert

Perhaps the most important word in Gina Jalbert's vocabulary is adapt.

Gina, of Arcadia, California, has become an expert at adapting. She also refuses to take no for an answer. Though she's used a wheelchair since she was 10 years old, it hasn't stopped her from pursuing her dreams.

Doctors diagnosed Gina with spina bifida when she was just an infant. People with spina bifida eventually lose the use of their legs. The doctors told Gina's parents that she would not be able to walk or lead a normal life. They even said she probably wouldn't graduate from high school.

Gina proved all of them wrong. She walked with leg braces until she was 10. When she could no longer walk, she began using a wheelchair. She quickly signed up for a wheelchair sports camp. She learned that people who use wheelchairs still can play many sports by adapting them. Her favorite wheelchair sport became tennis.

In wheelchair tennis, players get two bounces before they must hit the ball. Players also can score points if they hit their opponent's wheelchair with a ball. Otherwise, the rules are very similar to regular tennis. The speed with which wheelchair tennis players race around the court amazes most people.

Today, Gina is a five-time junior national wheelchair tennis champion. She won her first tournament when she was just 11 years old. That made her the youngest person ever to win that competition. Her victories have made her the number one ranked player in junior girls' wheelchair tennis. Now that she's older, Gina is competing in the women's division. The tournaments take her all over the U.S. from April to October. She practices almost every day to stay in shape and improve her skills.

Gina's next goal is to compete in the Paralympics in the year 2000. The Paralympics are like the Olympics, only the athletes play adapted sports. The games are held right after the regular Olympics. Gina also hopes to gain the number-one ranking for the women's division of wheelchair tennis.

Meanwhile, she has graduated from high school and is attending college. She is studying recreational therapy. Recreational therapists set up programs for people both with and without disabilities. Gina's goal is to bring disabled and able-bodied children together to play a sport. Besides having fun, they'll learn more about each other.

Gina believes that's important. She also believes it's easier now than it used to be. "People are more open now to individuals with disabilities," she says. "It used to be a child would see me in my wheelchair and ask their parent about it. The parent would often take the child away.

Now, they talk about it with them or with me. I'm willing to answer any questions a child might have."

Gina encourages young people to get to know people with disabilities. "Don't be afraid of how they look or act," she says. "Depending on the person, they may be willing to answer your questions. So don't be afraid to ask."

Gina also advises young people with disabilities to learn new ways to do what interests them. "You have to learn accessibility," she says. "If there's a barrier, you look for ways around it. There's nothing you can't do because there are ways to adapt to it. If you find something you want to do, find a way to adapt. Don't let anything stop you."

In addition to tennis, Gina competes in wheelchair basketball, weight lifting, racing, skiing, and badminton. She also enjoys reading, listening to all types of music, and participating in outdoor activities.

Get to know people ..... with disabilities.

 # Faith Vettrus

If you need a helping hand, just ask Faith Vettrus. Whether it's putting up walls, building bookshelves, or helping with homework, the Richfield, Minnesota teen is ready and willing.

Faith has always enjoyed working with other people. Sometimes, however, it's been tough. Faith has Attention Deficit Disorder. The disorder makes it hard for her to concentrate. It's also made her unpopular at times.

"Sometimes I'd get a little out of hand," Faith recalls. "I would be more excitable than the other kids. I'd get in a really silly mood. Many times the other kids would shy away from me. Up through eighth grade, I didn't have many friends."

Faith now takes medicine for the disorder. She says it's helped her a lot. Her experiences also have made her more understanding. When she was a freshman in high school, she spent lots of time with the upperclassmen. Now as a senior, she takes the time to talk to and help underclassmen. "It doesn't matter how old people are," she says. "We get along."

Faith works with older people, too. As a Girl Scout, she volunteers at a local nursing home. There, she helped build several sets of bookshelves. First she found grant money to pay for the bookshelves. Then she went out and bought the materials. She even spoke with local libraries and asked to buy any large-print books they were planning to sell. For her efforts, the Girl Scouts gave Faith their Silver Award. It's the second-highest award in Girl Scouting.

Faith received the Girl Scout "Silver Award" for building bookshelves at a nursing home.

Faith has done many other volunteer projects, too. She helped build homes for Habitat for Humanity. She ushered for the U.S. Olympic Festival. She helped teach elementary school children during summer school. She volunteered at a local nature center.

Faith stays involved in her high school as well. She is a peer counselor and plays in the school marching band. She also works with the school's theater program doing costumes, scenery and publicity. Even with all of her activities, Faith remains in the top five percent of her class, academically.

Faith's attitude about life is part of her success. "You have to keep moving, but you also need to stop and take a

look," she says. "If people really want to do something, they can find a way."

"It can be hard to do things because you may not have the money," she says. "Getting that money can mean you have to cut through a lot of red tape. But if you want to do something that seems worthwhile, you can find people willing to sponsor it."

Faith plans to go to college to study design communications. She wants to do computer-based graphic design for the movie industry and for TV commercials.

"You have to keep moving but you also need to stop and take a look."

How To Be A Hero

Have you ever thought about what it's like to have a disability? For people without disabilities, it's the first step toward understanding.

Try giving yourself a disability for an hour or two. Here are some suggestions.

- Put on a blindfold and experience how well you can get around your house. Then go to a library that carries books in braille. Close your eyes and run your fingers over the braille letters. How easy do you think it would be to read that way?

- Put in earplugs and see what life is like without sound. Try to read someone's lips to figure out what they're saying. Then, speak or sing into a tape recorder when you can't hear yourself. Do you sound different? You'll see why people who cannot hear, sound different from you when they speak. Check out a book on sign language. Learn a few words and phrases. Think what it would be like to talk like that all of the time.

- Sit in a wheelchair and see how well you can move it around. Next, take a trip to the store or the library. Pretend you can't walk up steps or up onto curbs. Can you find cuts in the curb? Ramps for wheelchairs? How about elevators? How would you get where you're going without them?

What do these experiences feel like to you? Imagine that you lived like that every day. Imagine the challenges you would face.

Not all disabilities are as obvious as these, however. Some people have developmental disabilities. Mental retardation is an example of a developmental disability. You may not know someone has this disability just by looking at them.

A developmental disability simply means the person who has it needs more help than you do to do some of the same things. It may take them longer to memorize a phone number. They may need help solving certain math problems. Maybe they need help to walk or to eat.

Like people with other disabilities, people with

developmental disabilities also want friends and fun things to do. In fact, it's important to remember that people with disabilities have most of the same needs as you do. They probably want friends as much as you do. They probably like the same books, games, and music as you do, too. Keep that in mind when you meet someone with a disability. Don't be scared of them. They're very much like you are. Talk to them and ask them questions.

Some places offer recreational or camping programs that bring disabled and able-bodied kids together. Try attending one. It's a great chance to make new friends. You'll also learn more about what it's like to live with a disability.

Above all, treat people with disabilities the way you would like to be treated. Be a friend. Be considerate. Don't be frightened just because they look, sound or act differently than you do.

If you have a disability, focus on what you can do, not what you can't do. You've just read stories about five young people who haven't let their disabilities stop them.

They have learned different ways to do what they want. So can you. Today, you also can take advantage of new technology to help you. Plus, there are many organizations that offer specialized help depending on the disability.

To find those organizations, start by asking your doctor. Many hospitals also have programs to help people with disabilities. Local community organizations, such as the United Way, may be able to help, too. Some will refer you to places that specialize in helping people with your disability. You can get the United Way phone number from your local phone book. Or, go to the library and ask the librarian for reference books listing organizations that help people with disabilities.

As these young people have shown, the only thing stopping you from your dreams is your own attitude!

Sign Language

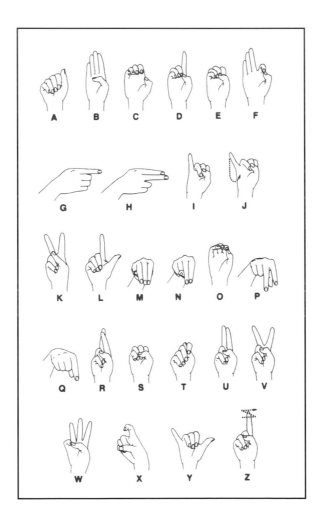

The one-hand manual alphabet is used as part of sign language to communicate with deaf persons.

GLOSSARY OF TERMS

adapted — to adjust an activity, such as a sport, to meet one's abilities.

Attention Deficit Disorder — a learning disorder that makes it hard to concentrate on things.

braille — a system of reading and writing that uses raised dots to represent letters.

cerebral palsy — A condition in which movement is impaired due to brain damage.

disability — any physical or mental condition that causes a person to be unable to do something he or she otherwise could do.

Judo — a type of martial art, like karate.

learning disability — one or more problems someone has that may interfere with schoolwork.

spina bifida — a condition in which people eventually lose the use of their legs.

syndrome — a group of symptoms that happen with a particular disease.

Index